CAR WORLD

500
600
700
800
1000
1200

CARLTON
KiDS

THIS IS A CARLTON BOOK
Text, design and illustration © Carlton Books Limited 2015

Published in 2015 by Carlton Books Limited
An imprint of the Carlton Publishing Group
20 Mortimer Street, London W1T 3JW

Design: Tall Tree
Cover Design: Ceri Hurst

10 9 8 7 6 5 4 3 2 1

A catalogue record for this book is available from the British Library.

ISBN: 978-1-78312-141-0
Printed in China

CAR WORLD

500
600
700
800
1000
04 17   1200
km

CLIVE GIFFORD

CONTENTS

⊕

Cars exert a grip on people like no other machine. They can be far more than just a convenient way of getting around. They excite, fascinate and inspire emotions in people – from the adrenalin rush of driving a high-performance car to the quiet pride in restoring a classic car from the past or the thrilling first glimpse of a car of the future.

This book is packed with a high-octane mix of some of the hottest cars around, from supremely stylish and iconic sports classics to the latest in full-throttle supercars and hypercars, incredible one-off designs and phenomenally fast record-breaking land vehicles. It looks at some of the most popular racing cars and the demands that competition places on their design and performance. It also looks forward to the advances in car design and technology that might be around the corner later in the 21st century.

Cars are raced in different ways, from multiple laps of the track and rallies across tough terrain to short, explosive runs along a straight drag strip. Top Fuel dragsters (right) are the fastest drag-strip vehicles of all, able to hit speeds above 500 km/h in seconds.

This Lamborghini Huracán is a high-performance supercar hand-built in Italy. Packed with innovative features, it has a top speed of more than 320 km/h.

Many cars are mass-produced in factories, but some are built by hand in small quantities or are one-off models. The Flatmobile (right) is a wacky one-off, built by British enthusiast Perry Watkins out of the parts of two Hillman Imp cars. Shaped like Batman's car, the open-topped vehicle is powered by an 875-cc engine and is the world's lowest roadworthy car (see page 47).

WHERE IT ALL BEGAN

The 19th century was a time of major breakthroughs in engineering. Among these were the first internal combustion engines, the first cars and many of the features of cars we take for granted today. Although inventors and pioneers existed elsewhere – especially in the United States, France and the UK – Germany, more than any other country, can lay claim to being the birthplace of the automobile.

FOUR-STROKE CYCLE

Nikolaus Otto was a travelling grocery salesman and self-taught engineer who tinkered with engine designs in the 1860s. Learning about Frenchman Alphonse Eugène Beau de Rochas's principles of a four-stroke engine, Otto perfected a petrol-fuelled engine in Cologne in 1876. It repeated the same four steps or strokes to provide power reliably. Otto's four-stroke cycle engine would be adopted by pioneering car makers.

The Mercedes 35 HP boasted a four-speed gearbox, pressed-steel chassis, foot-operated brakes and a top speed of 75–90 km/h.

 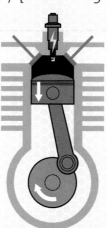  

A valve opens to let a mixture of fuel and air into the cylinder.

The piston rises to squeeze, or compress, the mixture.

A spark ignites the mixture, which expands, pushing the piston down.

As the piston rises again, it pushes waste gases out of the cylinder.

THE FIRST AUTOMOBILE

Karl Benz held patents for throttles and spark plugs before he built his first car in 1885 – a three-wheeler powered by a four-stroke internal combustion engine. The Benz Patent Motorwagen became the first car to go on sale in 1888, the same year that Benz's wife, Bertha, made the world's first long-distance car journey. Her 190-km drive from Mannheim to Pforzheim and back aroused massive interest and by 1900, Benz was the largest car maker in the world.

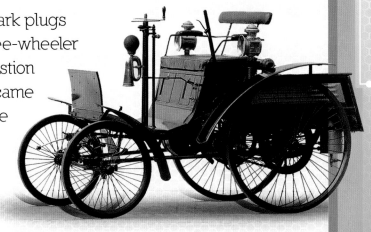

DAIMLER AND MAYBACH

In 1886 in Stuttgart, just 95 km down the road from Benz, Gottlieb Daimler (right) and Wilhelm Maybach fitted an Otto cycle engine to a stagecoach to produce the first petrol-engine four-wheeler. Fourteen years later, Maybach's Mercedes 35 HP (named after Mercédès Jellinek, the daughter of its first customer) helped usher in modern motoring with its longer, lower, lighter-weight design.

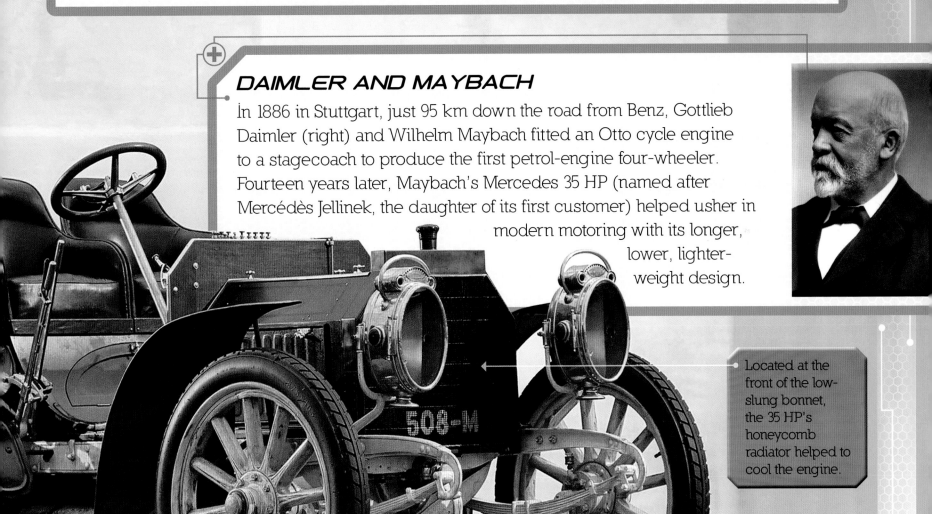

Located at the front of the low-slung bonnet, the 35 HP's honeycomb radiator helped to cool the engine.

POWER AND PRECISION

The internal combustion engine has grown up since the days of Otto, Benz and Daimler, but the core principles remain. Fuel and air are compressed and ignited inside an engine's cylinders. This creates rapidly expanding gases that push pistons. The fuel's chemical energy is converted into kinetic (moving) energy, which is transmitted to the axles and wheels of the car. Engineering innovations in the past 120 years have seen engines increase in power, performance and efficiency.

The biggest-capacity production car engine is the 8.4-litre, ten-cylinder engine fitted inside a 2015 Dodge Viper SRT supercar. This massive block generates around 645 hp.

BIG BLOCK

An engine's displacement, or capacity, is the volume inside all its cylinders. This is measured in litres or cubic centimetres. The smallest urban vehicles have 599-cc engines, while many small hatchbacks have 1.1- or 1.3-litre engines. A larger capacity with bigger or more cylinders means more fuel can be burned for each cycle of the engine, usually resulting in more power.

REFINEMENTS AND PRECISION

It's not just about the block and its size. Many other refinements can squeeze more power out of a car's engine. High-performance engines are often made from lighter parts, which need less energy to move them. Airflow into and out of the engine is carefully designed to meet as little resistance as possible. An improved exhaust system that channels waste engine gases away smoothly can add 10 horsepower (hp) or more to an engine's power.

ENGINE MANAGEMENT

Modern engine management systems use computers and sensors to monitor and adjust the precise workings of an engine, from varying the valve and ignition timing to controlling fuel injection into the cylinders. These systems can aid an engine to perform more efficiently in all conditions. Extra power can be generated by fitting an engine with turbochargers or superchargers, which force more air into the engine's cylinders.

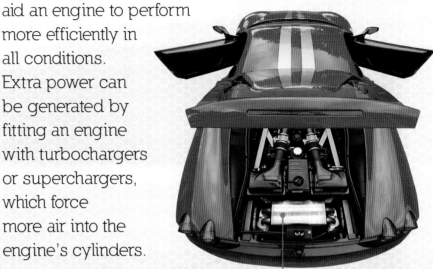

The Viper SRT can reach 100 km/h in just over three seconds and has a top speed of 330 km/h.

FOUR-FIGURE THRUST

Debuting in 2014, the Koennigsegg One:1 is fitted with an advanced aluminium block, 5-litre, V8 turbocharged engine. It can deliver an astonishing 1341 hp, more than two Formula One cars combined, making it the most powerful production road car engine around. As a result of engine power, slick aerodynamics and a rapid transmission system, the One:1 can race from 0–400 km/h in just 20 seconds.

GLOBAL CAR PRODUCTION

More than 65 million new cars are produced all around the world each year. Behind each new model lie many years of design, testing, revision and prototype building. CAD-CAM systems enable engineers to produce technical specifications for the thousands of parts that go into making a modern motor car.

Robot arms weld the frame of the car together with perfect accuracy. In a car like the A1's big brother, the A3 sedan, it takes 5,467 different spot weld points to construct the vehicle.

PARTS AND PROCESSES

A modern production line is a marvel of organization and choreography as cars are built and their additional parts – around 8,000 in the case of a BMW X6 car – fitted on a rolling assembly line in perfect harmony. Despite the rise of carbon fibre and composites in premium vehicles, most cars have a steel chassis and steel or aluminium body parts requiring large amounts of welding.

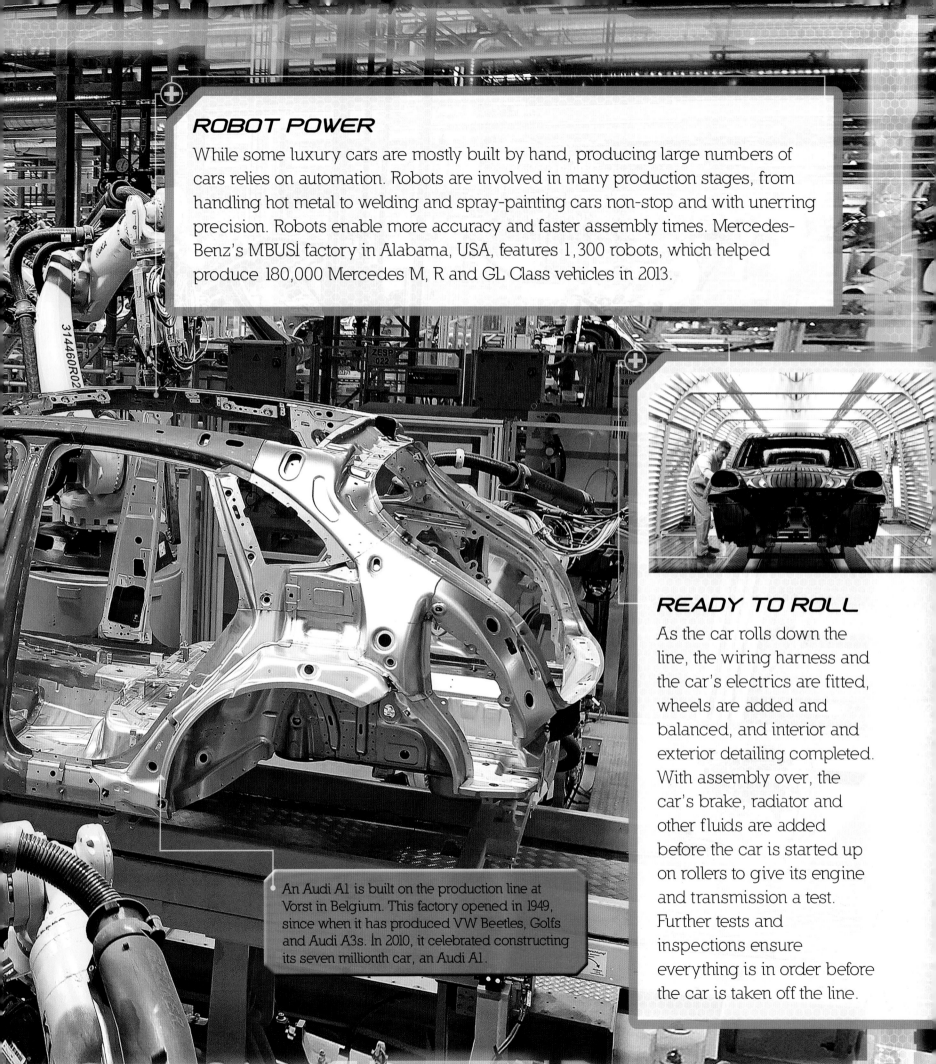

ROBOT POWER

While some luxury cars are mostly built by hand, producing large numbers of cars relies on automation. Robots are involved in many production stages, from handling hot metal to welding and spray-painting cars non-stop and with unerring precision. Robots enable more accuracy and faster assembly times. Mercedes-Benz's MBUSİ factory in Alabama, USA, features 1,300 robots, which helped produce 180,000 Mercedes M, R and GL Class vehicles in 2013.

READY TO ROLL

As the car rolls down the line, the wiring harness and the car's electrics are fitted, wheels are added and balanced, and interior and exterior detailing completed. With assembly over, the car's brake, radiator and other fluids are added before the car is started up on rollers to give its engine and transmission a test. Further tests and inspections ensure everything is in order before the car is taken off the line.

An Audi A1 is built on the production line at Vorst in Belgium. This factory opened in 1949, since when it has produced VW Beetles, Golfs and Audi A3s. In 2010, it celebrated constructing its seven millionth car, an Audi A1.

AUTOSTADT
Extreme car park

Welcome to car town! Volkswagen's Autostadt is an entire complex devoted to cars and their production, located next to the company's HQ in Wolfsburg, Germany. Each year, more than 1.2 million visitors come to marvel at the sight of the two Autotürme car towers. These 48-m-high glass silos are connected to the VW factory by an underground tunnel. Newly built vehicles are transported along the 700-m-long tunnel on automated rollers, then lifted by a robotic arm into a parking bay inside a silo. The parking process takes less than two minutes per car.

www.autostadt.de

TOP MARKS

Each 20-storey tower can store up to 400 vehicles awaiting collection or delivery. More than 35 per cent of all new VW cars built in Germany are collected from Wolfsburg by their owners. There is even a six-seat glass visitor 'car' that is lifted up through the silo and parked in a bay at the top of the tower.

A Volkswagen Golf is lifted high inside one of the Autotürme at VW's Wolfsburg plant at a speed of approximately 1.5 metres per second.

PERFORMANCE CARS

Slick, quick and with unrivalled handling, performance cars are the closest you can get on the road to the thrill of a racing car. As their name suggests, the emphasis is on speed, but not just top speed. Rapid acceleration, powerful braking and quick, responsive suspension provide the ultimate fast ride on roads. High performance increases the potential dangers, and manufacturers have developed pioneering safety measures for their fast cars using crash tests. These improvements have been rolled out to all forms of motor vehicle.

McLaren's innovative P1 supercar features a V8 petrol engine and an electric motor powered by 324 lithium-ion battery cells. The P1 can accelerate from 0–100 km/h in 2.8 seconds and has its top speed electronically limited to 349 km/h.

SPORTS CARS
Small and speedy

Sports cars offer exciting driving with better than everyday performance. They are usually lightweight vehicles with powerful engines and more advanced braking and suspension systems than regular hatchback and saloon cars. Many sports cars are two-door two-seaters, but some offer 2+2 seating with a pair of smaller seats in the rear.

This 2013 Boxster S has aluminium doors and bonnet, a top speed of 279 km/h and comes with either a six-speed manual gearbox or a seven-speed automatic transmission.

LOTUS EVORA

The Evora is the only current Lotus road car to come either as a two-seater or with 2+2 seating. Packing a Toyota V6 engine, which drives the rear wheels via a six-speed gearbox, the Evora has a top speed of more than 260 km/h and can reach 100 km/h from a standing start in under five seconds. Modified Evora cars have competed in a range of track competitions, including the Le Mans 24 Hours endurance race.

PORSCHE BOXSTER

The Boxster is an exciting two-seater sports car with its engine placed just behind the seats, and boots both at the front and rear of the car. The 2014 Boxster GTS model has a 3.2-litre engine generating 326 hp. This enables the car to go from 0–100 km/h in under five seconds – faster than some versions of its bigger brother, the Porsche 911.

MAZDA MX-5

The affordable Japanese MX-5 is the bestselling two-seater sports car in history. It first went on sale in 1990 and proved a huge hit, selling more than 920,000 by the end of 2013. The first version of this rear-wheel-drive car weighed only 940 kg, had a small 1.6-litre engine placed between the driver and front axle, and headlights that popped up from the car body. Later versions have added features – from airbags to precision gear changing – but remain faithful to the light, fun-to-drive design.

Large intakes just in front of the rear wheels channel cooling air into the engine compartment.

SPORTS CARS
Iconic and innovative

Sports car manufacturers vary greatly in size, from automotive giants such as Chevrolet, Toyota, Mercedes and BMW to smaller companies like Morgan, Yes! and Pagani who specialize in hand-building limited editions of their own car designs.

This 1963 Corvette Sting Ray features the classic 'fast back' sloping rear and weighs 1525 kg.

LONG-RUNNING CORVETTES

Into its seventh generation since its launch in 1953, Chevrolet's Corvette has long been one of the USA's most popular sports cars. The first 'Vettes' were convertibles with no outside door handles, meaning that people had to reach inside the car to open the doors. In 1963, the legendary Corvette Sting Ray was introduced with a fixed roof and split rear window. The seventh generation 2014 Corvette (above) has a powerful 455-hp engine, carbon fibre trim and a choice of six-, seven- or eight-speed gearbox.

BMW I8

A sports car with a twist, BMW's i8 is an electric hybrid with 96 battery cells powering its electric motor alongside a small, efficient, three-cylinder internal combustion engine. The i8 can be driven purely in electric motor mode up to speeds of 120 km/h. At higher speeds, the 1.5-litre engine can take over, boosting the car up to 250 km/h.

YES! ROADSTER

Some sports cars are sparse inside, while others are packed with luxury features. The Young Engineers Sportscar (Yes!) Roadster 3.2 Turbo has a very simple interior, but the car's suspension, and its seat and pedal position are customized for each owner. Buyers get to test out the aluminium-framed two-seater on a race track as part of their purchase.

With its distinctive bulges, the bonnet slopes at the front and features four hidden headlights. The lights roll upwards when required.

SUPERCARS
Performance plus

Exclusive and expensive, supercars push the boundaries of speed, performance and handling. Many can race from 0–100 km/h in under 3.5 seconds, have top speeds in excess of 300 km/h and are equipped with state-of-the-art handling, braking and driver aids. Recent models have included some of the finest supercars ever seen, including the Lamborghini Huracán, Ferrari 458 Speciale, the McLaren P1 and the Porsche 918 Spider. Competition between manufacturers is really hotting up.

The 2014 Lamborghini Huracán's V10 engine propels the supercar to speeds up to 320 km/h.

EARLY SUPERCARS

There is no one vehicle everyone agrees on as the first supercar, but many of the most likely contenders – from the Ford GT40 (below) to Ferrari's 250 GTO (pages 34–35) – had their origins as racing cars and were adapted for the road. Lamborghini's 1966 Miura (pages 42–43) was one of the first supercars to be designed from the start as a road car, but one with awesome performance.

PUSHING THE ENVELOPE

Supercars are at the cutting edge of car technology. They are often the first road cars to adopt innovations, such as carbon fibre bodies and active aerodynamics, originally developed for Formula One and other racing competitions. Some innovations can lead to unusual supercar features, like the periscope on the İsdera İmperator 108i to give the driver a rear view, or the six wheels on both the Covini CW6 and the Panther Six supercars.

Beneath the Huracán's angular styling is a carbon fibre and aluminium body shell and a seven-speed automatic gearbox.

HYBRID SUPERCARS

A number of the latest supercars feature both a powerful internal combustion engine and one or more electric motors to create a hybrid drive system, boost performance and offer the driver more control. Ferrari's LaFerrari supercar, for example, features a large 6.3-litre, V12 engine that generates 789 hp, but also includes an electric motor, which generates a further 161 hp.

BUGATTI VEYRON 16.4 SUPER SPORT
Extreme performance

Since its introduction in 2010, the Bugatti Veyron 16.4 Super Sport has been the world's fastest street-legal production car. With a price tag of around £1,700,000, this luxurious supercar offers technological innovation, enormous power and great speed in a hand-crafted package. The 100-litre fuel tank alone is made of 261 parts and takes three days to build.

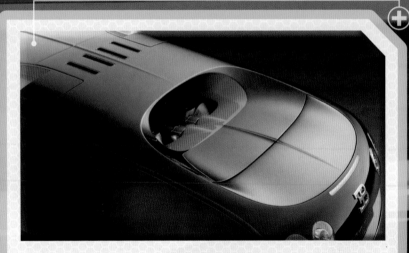

SUPER CYLINDERS

The Veyron's engine is a 16-cylinder beast with four turbochargers – devices that let more air into the cylinders during combustion to generate more power. The engine puts out 1,200 hp when turning at 6,400 revs per minute – an awesome amount of power. As a result, the Veyron Super Sport can accelerate from 0 to 100 km/h in just 2.5 seconds and reach 200 km/h in just 6.7 seconds. It has a top recorded speed of 431.072 km/h.

Air intakes channel air over the ceramic-carbon disc brakes. These measure 40 cm in diameter in the front, and 38 cm at the rear. They can stop the car from a speed of 100 km/h in just 2.4 seconds.

STICKING TO THE ROAD

With computer-controlled active suspension and an adjustable ride height that can drop the body to just 80–95 mm above the ground, the Veyron hugs the road even at high speeds. The adjustable rear spoiler deflects air to help create downforce, which makes the car grip the road. It can also rise to a 55° angle to act as an air brake.

Specially designed for the Veyron, these wide, slick Michelin tyres can run flat for up to 50 km without significant damage. Sensors for each tyre monitor air pressure and feed results back to the onboard computer.

Body panels are made of light, yet strong, carbon fibre. In normal ride mode, the Veyron measures 4.46 m long, 1.99 m wide and just 1.19 m high.

FAST FACT

The Veyron can go from zero to 200 km/h and brake to a standstill again in an unbelievably fast 12.5 seconds.

HYPER CARS
Pushing to the limit

Move over supercars, there is one small group of elite vehicles that outstrips them in performance and even in price. Hyper cars are made in small numbers. Their build and tuning are designed to extract the absolute maximum from new technology and available components. Cost is rarely an issue. Here are three of the most stunning examples currently on the road.

The Hennessey Venom GT uses sculpted carbon-fibre bodywork and an array of premium parts to keep its weight down to 1,244 kg. When paired with an engine that can deliver 1,200 hp, the result is an extremely fast hyper car. Over a distance of just 800 m, the Venom GT can go from standstill to 329.6 km/h!

A VENOMOUS RIDE

The Texas-built Hennessey Venom GT is based on a stretched, heavily modified Lotus Exige supercar chassis. This is fitted with a powerful Hennessey V8 engine, capable of generating 1,244 hp and launching the car from 0–300 km/h in just 13.63 seconds. In 2014, a Venom GT raced along a landing strip previously used for NASA's Space Shuttle. It reached an astonishing top speed of 435.31 km/h.

The Venom GT's rear wheels receive power via a six-speed gearbox. Carbon-ceramic disc brakes applied by six calipers per wheel give the car its stopping power.

LIGHT SPEED

Swedish manufacturer Koenigsegg introduced the stunning Agera R in 2011. The car features a host of innovations, including wheels made entirely of carbon fibre. These are about 40 per cent lighter than typical aluminium wheels. The entire vehicle weighs just 1,330 kg, but can travel at speeds of more than 400 km/h.

LOW RIDER

The low-slung Lamborghini Aventador LP700-4 is 4.78 m long but only 1.136 m high. Its V12 engine generates 700 hp, transmitted to all four wheels, giving the car rapid acceleration from 0–96 km/h in just 2.9 seconds. Its seven-speed gearbox is equally fast, enabling a change of gears in just 1/20th of a second.

The Aventador boasts upwards-opening scissor doors, a feature of the maker's top-end vehicles since the 1974 Lamborghini Countach.

CRASH!
Feeling the force

CRUNCH! A car hits a solid obstacle head-on at high speed. No need to call the emergency services – it's simply a crash test. Cars are tested rigorously as part of a manufacturer's safety programme. They are subjected to different types of impact – to the front, side and rear. They are also tested to see whether the car's frame can withstand rolling onto its roof and whether it channels the force of the impact away from passengers to aid their safety. High-speed cameras and sensor telemetry give engineers valuable data to analyse after each crash test.

A Toyota Crown sedan (left) takes part in an offset crash test of its front wing at a test centre in Susono, Japan. Offset tests are important because the crash impact is often as great as a front-on crash but concentrated onto a smaller area of the car.

BLOW UP!

In 1987, the Porsche 944, a performance car, was the first to be equipped with driver and passenger frontal airbags as standard. Airbags rapidly inflate when sensors detect the sudden increase in force as a crash occurs. Gases travel faster than 300 km/h to inflate a nylon bag that protects an occupant from head and chest impact injuries – all in 1/25th of a second!

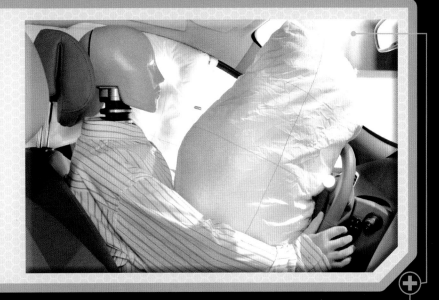

This Toyota Vitz hatchback is crashing into the Crown sedan. Images and data from both cars will show how the vehicles' bodies reacted to the intense crash forces.

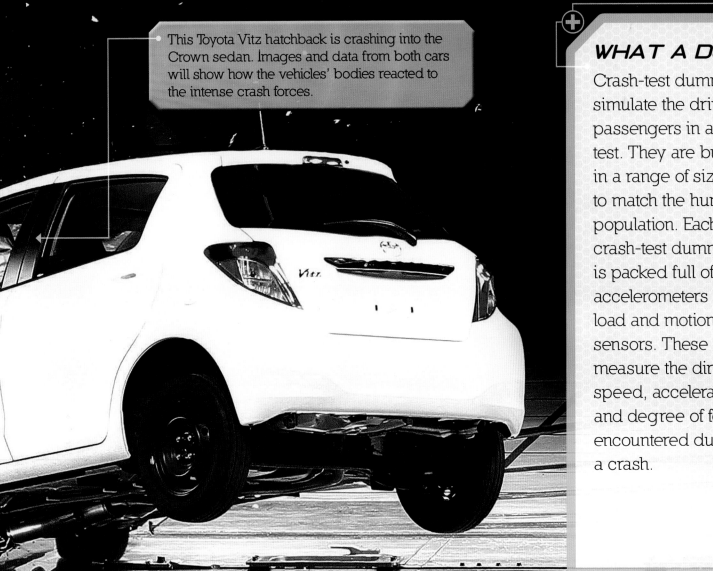

WHAT A DUMMY!

Crash-test dummies simulate the driver and passengers in a crash test. They are built in a range of sizes to match the human population. Each crash-test dummy is packed full of accelerometers and load and motion sensors. These measure the direction, speed, acceleration and degree of force encountered during a crash.

ICONIC CARS

Many cars are great successes, selling in large numbers or acquiring a reputation and value that makes an owner of one the envy of others. But only a handful of particularly special vehicles become a motoring icon – a vehicle that all petrolheads and even everyday car fans recognise and appreciate as deserving of special status. Models by the likes of Porsche, Mercedes, Ferrari and Jaguar have gone down in history as exceptional vehicles, known for their beauty, power and innovation.

The interior of this classic 1953 Chevrolet Bel Air has been carefully restored and now looks almost as good as new. Its iconic, early 1950s look, with a wide dashboard, a tissue dispenser, chrome detailing and a gear shift mounted on the steering column, has made the Bel Air very popular with modern car enthusiasts.

PORSCHE 911
Enduring performer

Little did Ferdinand 'Butzi' Porsche know when he was sketching out new designs for a successor to the Porsche 356 that he was creating a much-loved masterpiece. The Porsche 911 has rolled off production lines for more than 50 years – a record for a performance car that is unlikely ever to be beaten. More than 820,000 of this classic model have been made.

The 2014 Porsche 911 GT3 is ready for track racing or the road with a 0–96 km/h time of just three seconds.

ROAD AND RACING

Designed to hold four people, the Porsche 911 debuted at the Frankfurt Motor Show in 1963. It featured a rear-mounted, 2-litre engine, which was cooled by air drawn into the engine compartment by two fans, a 68-litre fuel tank and a top speed of 210 km/h. It proved a hit both on the road and at the track. Porsche 911s won both the Rally of Monte Carlo and the Daytona 24 Hours races four times, in addition to victories in Trans-Am and GT3 competitions.

TARGA TOP

In 1966, Porsche released its first 911 Targa. The word has gone on to name any vehicle with a roof that can be removed, leaving a permanent roll-bar-like structure running across the car above the back of the front seats. Other premium sports cars have since incorporated this in their design, including some versions of the Lotus Elise and Dodge Viper. Some 911 models in the 1990s featured a glass roof that could retract fully.

Twin Xenon headlights shine brightly on the outside, while inside, the driver sits in a seat made from carbon fibre.

THROUGH THE GENERATIONS

Over the decades, the 911 has received successive makeovers, but its distinctive coupé shape and rear-engine design have remained. Bumpers were changed from steel to aluminium in 1974, and to plastic in 1989. In 1997, the 996 model was the first to feature a water-cooled engine. Rear spoilers, which generate downforce to help the car grip the road, have come in many designs, from a fat 'whale tail' to a double-decker design and most recently a driver-adjustable active spoiler.

FERRARI 250 GTO
A true Italian stallion

A contender for the most beautiful car ever built, the Ferrari 250 GTO was designed to compete with the attractive new E-Type model by Jaguar, Ferrari's racing rival, which was unveiled in 1961. Ferrari's chief engineer, Giotto Bizzarrini, and later Mauro Forghieri, worked round the clock to design this awe-inspiring front-engined racer. With fewer than 40 manufactured, it is the most sought-after of all classic sports cars.

The 16.5-cm-wide rear wheels originally ran Dunlop racing tyres. The car's wheelbase is 4.33 m long and 2.4 m wide.

POWERPLANT

The 3-litre, V12 engine was developed from the powerful and reliable Tipo 168/62 that propelled Ferrari's 250 Testa Rossa. Fitted close to the ground to keep the bonnet low, it could develop 290–300 hp. The power was transmitted to the rear wheels through a five-speed gearbox that was unusual at the time. Waste engine gases ran out of four rear exhaust pipes.

BUILDING BASICS

The car's sumptuous curves, styled by Sergio Scaglietti, were formed from aluminium body panels covering a tubular steel frame. Inside the car the simple cockpit had no carpet, bare instruments and no fan, just inlets to channel air into the car.

CHAMPION RACER

The car's aerodynamics, honed during wind-tunnel testing at the University of Pisa, along with its light weight (880 kg) helped give the 250 GTO a 0–96 km/h time of under 6 seconds and a top speed of 280 km/h. It was built as a road car but its real home was the racing track. The 250 GTO won many races, including class wins at Le Mans in 1962 and 1963, the Nürburgring 1000 km in 1963 and 1964, and three Targa Florias.

Shaped plexiglass covers over the headlights improved airflow.

Three D-shaped panels on the nose could be removed to increase the amount of cooling air reaching the radiator.

THE VW BEETLE
Surf's up

The world's most popular car was launched in 1938 and continued in production until 2003, by which time more than 21.5 million had been built. The car's distinctive, curved design, along with its simple mechanics and affordable price, made the Volkswagen Beetle a firm favourite with millions of motorists.

In 1997, Volkswagen launched their New Beetle, a completely different front-wheel-drive car.

THE PEOPLE'S CAR

In 1934, the Austrian car designer Ferdinand Porsche was entrusted by the German government with the tough task of creating a *Volkswagen* or 'people's car'. This was to be a cheap, reliable vehicle that could carry a family of five on Germany's new motorway network with good fuel economy. Porsche's design went on sale in 1938 for little more than the cost of a motorcycle, but mass production only began after the Second World War.

Luggage could be stored both underneath the bonnet and behind the rear seat. Some models had a fold-down rear seat.

STEP–BY–STEP INNOVATIONS

Original Beetles boasted some surprising features – from rear-mounted, air-cooled engines to a cabin air heater, which channelled hot air from the engine, but in other aspects they were crude. The cars had painted metal interiors, cable-operated brakes, no fuel gauge and 25-hp engines. From the 1940s onwards, a staggering 78,000 changes were made to the design, parts and workings, but the 'bug-like' body shape remained.

A series of hit movies about a 1963 VW Beetle, called Herbie, began with the 1969 film *The Love Bug*.

MAJOR MILESTONES

Beetle sales soared in the 1950s and 1960s, with convertible models introduced, and modified versions built for off-road racing. A two-seater sports model was built in the 1950s and a larger Super Beetle was launched in 1971. Production ended in Germany in 1978, but continued in Brazil until 1986 and Mexico until 2003, six years after Volkswagen launched its New Beetle – a completely different front-wheel-drive car.

Rear engine provided rear-wheel drive and a top speed, in the original models, of about 100 km/h.

The car's original windscreen washer system avoided an expensive electric motor by using pressurized air from the car's overinflated spare tyre, stored under the bonnet.

FORD MUSTANG
American hustle

The Ford Mustang is an American icon. It was the original 'pony' car – an affordable, compact vehicle with sleek looks and sports performance. On its launch day in 1964, 22,000 Mustangs were ordered and a record one million were sold in two years. Mustangs have been owned by movie stars, racing drivers and American presidents (Bill Clinton). Modern versions of the Mustang are still made today.

THROUGH THE GENERATIONS

Over the decades the Mustang has evolved several times, to include redesigned bodywork and new engines. The fastest early Mustang, the 1969 Boss 429, sprinted from zero to 96 km/h in just 5.3 seconds, with its engine generating up to 375 hp. A fifth-generation Mustang, the 2013 Shelby GT 500, had a 5.8-litre V8 engine that boasted 662 hp and took the car from zero to 96 km/h in only 3.5 seconds.

The long, sloping hood of the the original Mustang had a dropped radiator grille on which was placed the galloping horse symbol – the iconic logo of the Mustang brand.

The all-steel body was originally available in 15 different colours.

SUPER STUNTS

In 1966, Ford publicized the Mustang by building one on the observation deck of New York's Empire State Building. They pulled the same stunt in 2014 to launch a new convertible (left). A 1968 Mustang GT 390 starred in the action movie *Bullitt*, where it featured in an epic, 10-minute-long car chase.

This 1968 Mustang 428 Cobra Jet had a top speed of 204 km/h. The 2013 Shelby GT 500 Mustang's top speed is in excess of 305 km/h.

RACING COLOURS

Ever since one was used as a pace car at the 1964 Indianapolis 500, Ford Mustangs and speed racing have gone hand in hand. They have been raced on roads, across rough ground and in rallies. In 2011, Mustangs took part in the Nationwide Series of NASCAR races for the first time.

MERCEDES-BENZ 300SL
Sport light, sport fast

One of German motoring's finest hours came in 1954 at the New York International Auto Show. There, Mercedes-Benz debuted its brand-new Sport Leicht (sport light) coupé car, the 300SL. From its striking red-leather interior to its sculpted lines and amazing doors, the 300SL wowed car fans there and all over the world.

Chassis rises up to the driver's knees, so the car has a foldable steering wheel to aid entering and exiting.

RACING HERITAGE

In 1952, Mercedes returned to motor racing for the first time since the Second World war. Their W194 car had an engine from the rather unsporty Mercedes Type 300 Adenauer sedan, yet the racer was a design triumph. It featured a lightweight, tubular metal chassis; plastic instead of glass windows, and astonishing gull-wing doors that pivoted up and out from hinges on the car's roof. The W194 won the five-day Carrera Panamericana race and was the first German car to win the Le Mans 24 Hours endurance race.

A lighter, all-aluminium body was available on request, at extra cost.

FUEL INJECTION

In 1954, Mercedes developed a road-going version of the W194 – the 300SL. It still had gull-wing doors but was now fitted with a 130-litre fuel tank and a six-cylinder engine, with direct fuel injection. This was a first for production road cars and gave the 300SL 45 hp more than W194 as well as a top speed of over 240 km/h.

Hydraulic struts open the gull-wing doors, which do not feature wind-down windows – just small quarter panels that can be opened to let in air.

ROADSTER

Mercedes introduced an open-topped roadster version of the 300SL in 1957. The gull-wing doors were replaced with regular side doors and a substantial redesign was given to the car's rear suspension, chassis and cockpit instruments. Its fuel-tank capacity was reduced by 30 litres to create additional boot space. The car proved popular, especially in the United States.

LAMBORGHINI MIURA
Pioneering supercar

After he was snubbed by Enzo Ferrari when he asked for improvements to his Ferrari 250, Italian tractor maker Ferruchio Lamborghini set about taking on Ferrari and other leading sports car manufacturers. He formed a company in 1963 to build luxury grand-touring saloon cars, starting with the 350 GT in 1964. The following year, a team led by Lamborghini's head engineer Gian Pollo Dallara put the company on the map and changed sports car design for ever. Their car was called the Miura.

Deep, swept-back windscreen rises to the roof top, which is only 105 cm from the ground.

The Miura's headlights popped up when in use and sat flush to the bodywork when not. They were taken from a Fiat 850 – a small, simple coupé.

THE P400 PROJECT

The Miura began life as the P400 project, built around a powerful V12 engine. It was the engine's position that was revolutionary. Up to then, only racing cars tended to have mid-engined designs, with the engine immediately behind the seats. The Miura matched this, but in a road-going production vehicle. To keep the car shorter, the engine was turned sideways – known as transverse mounting.

The Miura's V12 engine had a capacity of 3,929 cc and could deliver up to 350 hp. It shared its lubrication system with the car's gearbox.

SLEEK LINES

With a sleek, rounded body shape from 25-year-old designer Marcello Gandini, the Miura looked sharp and had performance to match. Although wild to handle in some situations, its top speed of 270 km/h and 0–100 km/h in under 6.8 seconds made it one of the fastest cars around at the time. More than 750 Miuras were built in three main versions until 1972, when it was replaced by the more angular Countach, which again boasted a body design by Marcello Gandini. By that time, a trend for mid-engined exotic sports cars had been set, inspired by Lamborghini's first supercar.

JAGUAR E-TYPE
British classic

The most stylish sports car to come out of the UK, the E-Type (or XKE in the US) was described by the great Enzo Ferrari as 'the most beautiful car ever made' when he saw it at its debut at the 1961 Geneva Motor Show. With an on-the-road price of just over £2,097 for the basic model, the E-Type was much cheaper than the sports cars of Italian manufacturers Ferrari and Maserati, and orders flooded in.

The rear of the car tapered away smoothly with twin exhausts mounted in the middle and with a side-opening boot door.

BODY WORKS

The E-Types's unusually smooth, sweeping lines and long, sculpted nose were the work of Jaguar's Malcolm Sayer. He was a mathematician and specialist in aerodynamics who had previously worked for aircraft companies. He had used a monocoque body design on his previous Jaguar vehicle, the D-Type racing car that won a hat-trick of Le Mans 24 Hours victories (1955, 1956 and 1957).

The 4.45-m-long body began with a low-profile radiator air inlet, but with no place to put a licence plate. Instead, owners had to put a sticker across the low bonnet.

SERIES ONE AND TWO

Available as a coupé or open two-seater, the car came with independent rear suspension, disc brakes and either a 3.8- or 4.2-litre, six-cylinder engine. Acceleration was brisk at 0–100 km/h in seven seconds, and a top speed of more than 240 km/h made it one of the most rapid road cars of its time. Series Two E-Types (from 1968) featured bigger bumpers, a larger front air inlet, power steering and air conditioning options.

RACING E-TYPES

The E-Type was designed as a road car, not a racing car but some owners inevitably took their cars racing. Jaguar had officially withdrawn from motorsport in 1956, but the company helped owners to prepare their cars and even produced a few lightweight, aluminium-bodied cars for the track. E-Types like this early model are still raced today at historic racing events.

CRAZY CARS

Throughout automotive history, many odd vehicles have turned heads due to their outrageous design or construction. Some were built for fun, as a challenge or were produced to attract attention. Other seemingly crazy cars were serious attempts to push the envelope and innovate in order to come up with something startlingly new. These include flying cars, amphibious vehicles which are able to traverse land and water, and attempts to create the very fastest land vehicles of all. Make no mistake, from racing sofas to 26-wheeled stretched limousines, there are some truly wild rides out there!

Just 48.26cm tall, Flatmobile is the world's lowest-slung roadworthy car. Built by Perry Watkins from two Hillman Imps, the Flatmobile is based on Batman's vehicle and features a homemade jet engine built from a turbocharger originally from a large Volvo F10 truck.

WEIRD WHEELS
Attention-grabbing autos

Many vehicles command attention when they cruise past due to their sleek racing lines or head-turning engine sounds. Others boggle the eyes and mind due to their extreme design or size.

Behind the tinted windows, the passengers enjoy a powerful sound system, videos on TV screens, a bar and a fridge to serve cold drinks.

STRETCHING IT OUT

Stretch limos carry partygoers around town. Most are made by lengthening the wheelbase and adding body sections in order to extend a limousine or a utility vehicle, such as a Hummer H2. Others take a more surprising car as a starting point for a stretch conversion. Built in Los Angeles, the Mini XXL is based on a Mini Cooper S but fitted with an extra set of wheels to help support its 6-m-long body. The car even contains a working hot tub.

This pink stretch limo, on the streets in Russia, started life as a 5.17-m-long Hummer H2 sports utility vehicle. It has been stretched to almost double the length, and accommodates 16 seats.

SUPER-SIZED

The largest stretch limo was Jay Ohrberg's 30.5-m-long, 26-wheeler American Dream, which contained a swimming pool and bed. The largest four-wheeler is a Dodge Power Wagon replica (right), built for Sheikh Hamad bin Hamdan Al Nahyan of the United Arab Emirates. Eight times the size of the original, it weighs around 50 tonnes and contains four bedrooms.

The Peel P50's 49-cc engine generates just 3.4 hp yet can propel the car to 60 km/h.

PINT-SIZED P50

The 1962 Peel P50 was the world's smallest production car. In 2011, a new version went on sale. Measuring just 1.37 m long, 1.04 m wide and 1.2 m high, the microcar has just one door, one wiper and no reverse gear. At about 60 kg, it can be pulled by hand into a parking space.

TRANSFORMER

When is a car not a car? When it's a cycle car. This cross between a car and a bike has three wheels, seating for two, a six-speed gearbox and a steering wheel like a car. But its 160-hp engine drives a large rear wheel via a chain like a motorbike, giving the 470-kg machine a top speed of 210 km/h.

ONE-OFF WONDERS
Mad machines

Testaments to the car-maker's art, one-off vehicles can be wacky, weird and wonderful. Some, such as colourful hot rods, are revamps of old cars, while others, such as the Blastolene Special, re-use old components in a brand new body. The Blastolene packs the transmission system from a Greyhound bus and the huge 810-hp engine from an M47 Patton Tank into a custom-built aluminium body.

This demented dining table car, complete with candles, plates and chairs, was built from the chassis and parts of a Reliant Scimitar Sabre car. Named Fast Food, it raced at the Santa Pod dragster strip in 2010.

HOT RODS

Serious customizing of cars began with hot rods. These are vintage roadster cars, such as Ford Model Ts and Model As from the 1920s–40s, stripped down, fitted with large engines and finished with eye-catching paint jobs. Other cars, though not considered hot rods by purists, have been customized in similar fashion, and include VW Beetles and 1950s Chevys.

SIX-WHEELED SPEEDSTER

While several teams, including Williams and Ferrari, have built six-wheeled Formula One cars, only one car made it to a Grand Prix start line – the Tyrrell P34. Its four small front wheels were designed to increase grip when cornering and reduce the drag that would come from a single pair of larger front wheels. The P34 was relatively successful, winning the 1976 Swedish Grand Prix.

The P34 weighed 575 kg and the front of the car ran on four 25-cm-diameter wheels.

RECORD-BREAKING RIDES

Strange cars have been constructed in order to break world records. These include the world's lowest car, the Flatmobile (see page 47) and the world's smallest roadworthy car called Wind Up. Built by Perry Watkins out of a child's coin-operated ride, Wind Up measures just 66 cm wide. It is powered by a 150-hp engine from a Shanghai Shenke quad bike. The entire body lifts up to allow a driver to enter and exit the vehicle.

L789 HOC

Under the tablecloth is a Rover V8 engine. This powers the mad machine to an extremely rapid 183 km/h.

AIR AND WATER
Cars that can fly or float

Some cars aren't just at home on roads or off-road trails, they can also head into water or take off and fly through the air. Most of these extraordinary vehicles are experimental or pre-production models, but some have been built commercially in significant numbers.

On water, the Panther's engine powers its jet thruster technology. This sucks in water and expels it out behind to push the vehicle forwards. The vehicle is powerful enough to tow a waterskier or wakeboarder.

ON THE WATER

Developed from of the troop carriers of World War II, the first production amphibious car, the 1961 Amphicar Model 770, had a Triumph Herald engine and a modest 13 km/h top speed on the water. The Gibbs Aquada (above) can whizz across lakes at 56 km/h. It is powered by a jet thruster that sucks up water and then propels it out behind the car.

WATERCAR PANTHER

Powered by a Honda Acura 3.7-litre engine that generates 305 hp, the WaterCar Panther can reach speeds of over 120 km/h on land and 60 km/h on water. A hydraulic suspension system allows the Panther to be driven into the water, with the wheels then retracting up into the body in under eight seconds. The Panther holds four passengers and costs around US$120,000.

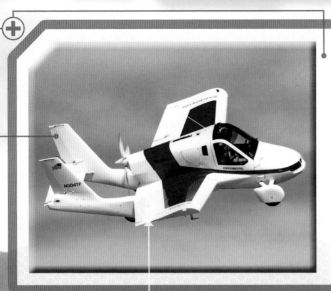

IN THE AIR

Drive to the airport and take off in the same vehicle – that's the purpose of the Terrafugia Transition. Its foldable wings take only a minute to assemble, with electric motors and electromagnets locking parts into place. On the road, the Transition's Rotax 912iS engine delivers 100 hp to give a top speed of 105 km/h. In the air, the engine powers a pusher propeller at the rear, allowing it to fly at 160 km/h, with a maximum range of 660 km.

The cockpit seats two people and has both a steering wheel and a control stick.

The SkyRunner has a three-cylinder, 114-hp engine and an 800-km range on the road. Its fuel levels and speed can be checked using an iPad attached to the dashboard.

CHUTE CARS

Several cars forego wings in favour of a hang-glider sail. Parajet's SkyRunner, for example, can soar at 320 km/h at altitudes of over 4,000 m, suspended underneath its paragliding wing-like chute. On the road, the buggy-like car, with its fibreglass and carbon bodywork, weighs only 420 kg. It can reach speeds of over 180 km/h and race from 0–100 km/h in just 4.3 seconds.

The 4.6-m-long Jeep-like body is waterproof, and constructed out of fibreglass. It is fitted over a chromoly steel frame and filled with Styrofoam, which aids buoyancy.

THE FASTEST
Blink and you'll miss them

Since the development of the very first cars, people have been obsessed with speed. Some have pushed their vehicle to its limit to find out how fast it could go. The world land speed record is the ultimate measure. Vehicles attempting to break this record must make two runs over a set distance within one hour. Their speed is taken as their average speed over both runs.

PIONEERING RECORD HOLDERS

The record has been overtaken more than 35 times since Gaston de Chasseloup-Laubat reached 63.15 km in an electric car in 1898. Just 11 years later, Victor Hémery broke the 200 km/h barrier, driving a Blitzen Benz (left). The record soared in the 1960s as jet engines replaced internal combustion engines. These jet-powered cars, such as Craig Breedlove's Spirit of America and Gary Gabelich's Blue Flame, relied on raw thrust rather than the engine directly turning the wheels.

THRUST SSC

In 1997, Thrust SSC set a new land speed record, roaring to an average speed of 1,227.985 km/h, making it the first car to break the sound barrier. The 16.5-m-long vehicle was powered by two large Rolls Royce Spey engines more commonly found in Phantom fighter-bomber aircraft. These consumed 18 litres of fuel per second – equal to an average car using approximately 55 litres to travel one kilometre.

FUTURE RECORD BREAKERS

A number of teams are striving to break Thrust's record – including Thrust's driver, Andy Green, and team leader Richard Noble. Their new Bloodhound SSC, under development, aims to become the first car to go faster than 1,000 mph (1,600 km/h).

Bloodhound will be powered by three different engines. A petrol engine from a supercar will drive pumps in the vehicle, while a Eurojet EJ200, normally found in a Eurofighter military jet, will propel the vehicle to a speed of around 500 km/h. At that point, a Nammo rocket engine will take over. With its engines combined, Bloodhound SSC will have as much power as 180 Formula One cars!

Made of aluminium, Bloodhound's 91-cm-wide wheels will revolve at up to 10,000 times a minute to achieve the record-breaking speed.

Bloodhound is predicted to accelerate from zero to 1,600 km/h in just 55 seconds, completing its timed mile (1.6 km) in just 3.6 seconds!

RACING CARS

Ever since cars were first built, they have been raced, testing not only the driver's skill and courage but also the vehicle's design, performance, reliability and durability. Racing has developed into a wide range of different classes and events – from short, sharp dragster sprints that are over in seconds to endurance races many hours long and rallies that can last weeks at a time. Each form of racing demands a different type of vehicle – from souped-up saloons for touring car competitions and robust offroad performers for rallies, to lightning fast and slick single-seaters for open-wheel categories such as IndyCar and Formula One.

Ryan Hunter-Reay leads the field as he races his IndyCar at the 2014 Grand Prix of Long Beach. IndyCars are fast, light, open-wheel cars that are raced on tracks around North America. They are fuelled by ethanol and can reach top speeds of around 360 km/h.

NASCARS
America's favourite racing

NASCAR races are fast, furious contests between as many as 40 cars. They can be between 465 km and 970 km long and are raced over multiple laps of a track. NASCAR's early years used stock cars – vehicles straight off the production line. Today, the three manufacturers that compete in NASCAR's Sprint Cup – Ford, Chevrolet and Toyota – produce heavily modified race vehicles.

The toughened gas tank holds around 67 litres of racing fuel, which contains around 15 per cent ethanol.

GEN-6

The latest Generation 6 (Gen-6) NASCARs first raced at the 2013 Daytona 500. The cars are more than 70 kg lighter than the previous model, partly due to a bonnet made of carbon fibre instead of steel. Gen-6 are the first NASCARs with fuel injection, and their cast- iron block engines generate up to 850 hp to give a top speed of about 300 km/h.

With no doors, drivers enter and exit through the windows which, during racing, are covered in a nylon mesh netting to keep the driver inside the car should it crash.

IN THE PITS

During races, pit stops allow for a change of tyres, refuelling and repairs. A team of six pitmen descend on the car, with the jackman raising it off the ground, wheelmen replacing wheels, and a gas man who tops up the tank using 45-litre dump cans of fuel. Through sharp teamwork, a NASCAR pit stop can be completed in 12 seconds or less.

SAFETY FEATURES

A NASCAR's roof is a busy place. It contains an exit hatch if the driver cannot get out of the window, a TV camera that relays the race to fans from the car's point of view, and roof flaps that lift, deflect air and help keep the car on the ground should it go into a spin. Inside the cab, a sturdy roll cage made of metal tubing protects the driver if the car flips or rolls.

RALLY RACERS
Whatever the weather

The World Rally Championship (WRC) is the pinnacle of rally racing. Each of the 13 rallies on its annual calendar poses massive challenges to the car, driver and co-driver. On one stage, they may be battling through rutted tracks, hills and ditches or loose gravel trails. On another, they may have to contend with mud, slippery snow and ice, or plough through water crossings.

EVERY SECOND COUNTS

WRC rallies are held all over the world, from Mexico to Australia. Each rally has a number of stages – timed sections that must be completed as quickly as possible. Cars are timed to a tenth of a second and the top ten drivers in each rally are awarded points that go to the season's end total. This decides which manufacturer and which driver are crowned champions.

Tyres are 46 cm in diameter and 20 cm wide for smooth asphalt or tarmac stages, or 38 cm in diameter and 17.5 cm wide for racing over loose material such as gravel.

An inlet above the windscreen channels air into the cabin to cool driver and co-driver as they race in a car propelled by a straight four-cylinder engine generating 300 hp.

The VW Polo R WRC is 3.98 m long, 1.82 m wide and 1.36 m high. Road-ready but without the driver and co-driver, the car has a minimum weight of 1,200 kg.

PRODUCTION PLUS

All cars that compete in the WRC are based on production models, but WRC versions are hugely modified during hundreds of hours of rebuilding work. All excess weight is removed; the body and chassis are made stiffer and stronger to deal with the tough conditions; and specialist rally cockpit seats, suspension systems and other parts are added. The rules specify a 1.6-litre engine size as maximum.

Instead of a simple roll cage, driver and co-driver are protected by a safety cell made up of 50 m of strong steel pipe that is welded into place.

PIONEERING RECORD HOLDERS

Volkswagen Motorsport competed in WRC rallies in 2011 and 2012 using modified Škoda Fabia S2000 cars, but used a new vehicle in 2013 – the Volkswagen Polo R WRC. After 18 months of development and thousands of test kilometres to refine the aerodynamics and handling, the car debuted at the 2013 WRC Rally of Monte Carlo, finishing second. Sébastien Ogier and co-driver Julien Ingrassia proved unstoppable that year, winning nine of the 13 rallies to be crowned champions.

FORMULA ONE
Tearing up the track

Formula One (F1) features the highest-performance track racing cars in the world. No expense is spared to build, test and refine these speed demons. They can race at 320 km/h, accelerate from zero to 100 km/h in under three seconds, and brake hard from a lightning-fast 300 km/h to a standstill in under four seconds.

Driver sits in a cockpit protected by roll bars and a light but tough safety cell, which also encloses the flexible fuel tank.

Flaps in the back wing open when a car's DRS (drag reduction system) is in operation. This reduces a car's downforce but increases its top speed by around 15 km/h to aid overtaking.

AN F1 TEAM

Pairs of F1 cars are designed and run by teams (11 in 2014) throughout a race season. The vehicles are made up of more than 70,000 parts, each of which must withstand the extreme conditions found in F1 racing. The F1 car steering wheel, for example, is a complex electronic instrument, with paddles for the car's eight-speed gearbox and controls to alter brake, engine and fuel consumption, among many other functions.

Since the 2014 season, each car has used a turbocharged 1.6-litre V6 engine. This generates around 650 hp, with its revs limited to 15,000 rpm.

RACE WEEKEND

Each F1 Grand Prix race begins with practice sessions around the track, which are followed by an intense qualifying period in which drivers try to record the fastest lap time in order to get as high a position on the starting grid as possible. The start of F1 races can be dramatic, with cars powering off the grid to gain places before the first corner is reached. Throughout the race, team tactics come into play as drivers seek to conserve fuel and tyre wear while racing as hard as they can.

FEEL THE FORCE

The car's body and wings generate downforce to help the car grip the track and give it phenomenal cornering ability. F1 cars can race at 300 km/h around the fastest corners where even the best supercars would have to slow considerably. This sort of cornering, as well as rapid acceleration and braking, generates severe G-forces on the driver.

The 2014 F1 runner up, Nico Rosberg, powers his Mercedes F1 car around the Monaco race circuit. F1 drivers like Rosberg must make 2,500–4,000 gear changes in every race.

AUDI R18 E-TRON QUATTRO
Instant Le Mans legend

Built for speed, hour after hour, the sleek, beautiful and technologically innovative Audi R18 e-tron quattro became an endurance-racing sensation when it debuted in 2012. Its powerful 3.7-litre V6 engine and streamlined aerodynamics enable the car to reach speeds of over 320 km/h – but there's more inside that makes it a winner.

A digital rearview mirror uses cameras that project images onto the driver's mirror to give him a wide, clear sight of the view behind.

IT'S ELECTRIC

Hybrid cars are powered by a regular internal combustion engine coupled with an electric motor. The R18's turbocharged engine runs on diesel fuel and generates up to 515 hp, but the car also features a motor generator unit (MGU). Energy recovered from the car as it brakes is converted into electricity that powers the MGU, which drives the front axle and wheels.

Carbon fibre is used extensively in the R18, allowing its weight to be kept down – just 900 kg for its debut race. The hybrid drive system saves weight too, as it consumes less fuel per kilometre and allows for a smaller fuel tank – just 58 litres – than in previous Audi endurance cars.

CHAMPION RACER

The R18 e-tron quattro became the first hybrid car to win the Le Mans 24 Hours race in 2012, completing 378 laps in the full day and night of racing and covering a staggering 5,151.8 km.

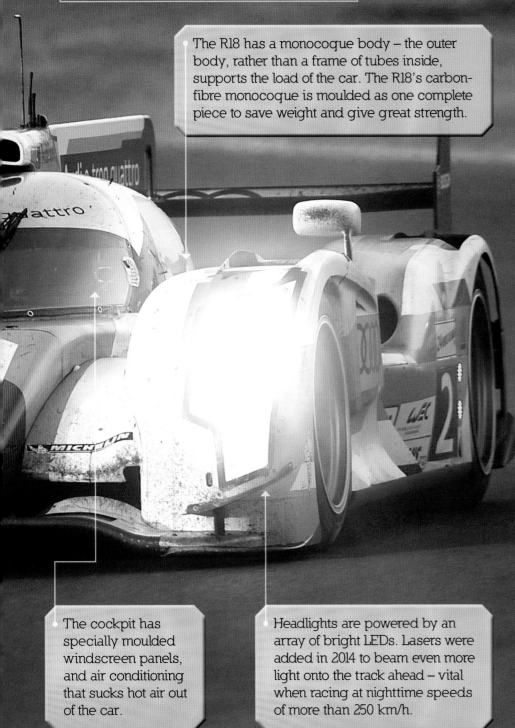

The R18 has a monocoque body – the outer body, rather than a frame of tubes inside, supports the load of the car. The R18's carbon-fibre monocoque is moulded as one complete piece to save weight and give great strength.

LE MANS 24 HOURS

The most famous endurance race, the 24 Hours of Le Mans, was first held in 1923 and is now raced on the 13.65-km-long Circuit de la Sarthe. The undulating track has many famous features, including the twisting L'Arche Chicane and the pulsating Mulsanne Straight. Cars can exceed 300 km/h before heavy braking slashes speeds to below 70 km/h at the tight Mulsanne corner.

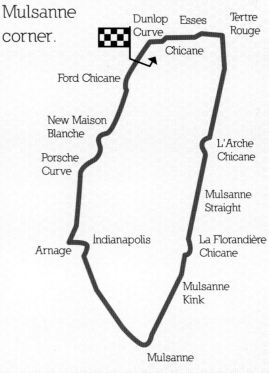

Dunlop Curve
Esses
Tertre Rouge
Chicane
Ford Chicane
New Maison Blanche
Porsche Curve
L'Arche Chicane
Mulsanne Straight
Arnage
Indianapolis
La Florandière Chicane
Mulsanne Kink
Mulsanne

The cockpit has specially moulded windscreen panels, and air conditioning that sucks hot air out of the car.

Headlights are powered by an array of bright LEDs. Lasers were added in 2014 to beam even more light onto the track ahead – vital when racing at nighttime speeds of more than 250 km/h.

OFF-ROAD WARRIORS
Any terrain, any time

The Dakar Rally is the world's most famous and perhaps most demanding long-distance race. Held over almost three weeks across 8,000 km or more of tough terrain, it places demands on the driver, co-driver and vehicle like no other competition. Vehicles have to be incredibly reliable, able to cross sand dunes, rugged rock pavements, loose dirt trails and deep water, all without losing traction or stopping for time-consuming repairs. To show just how tough a test the Dakar is, only 204 of the 431 vehicles that started the 2014 race completed it.

TOUAREG'S THREE IN A ROW

Volkswagen's Touareg SUV, modified for off-road racing, has proved a top Dakar performer. Its 2.5-litre, five-cylinder diesel engine with twin turbochargers sits inside a tough chassis made of aircraft-grade steel. Inside, there's plenty of space for driver and co-driver, navigation equipment, two spare wheels, tools and water supplies. In 2009, the Touareg became the first diesel-powered car to win the Dakar. It followed up with wins in 2010 and 2011.

VW Race Touareg is covered in body panels made of carbon fibre and Kevlar – a material used in body armour. A large inlet on the front of the roof filters air, removing sand and dust particles, before it flows into the cabin.

MINI MAGIC

Successor to the Touareg's Dakar crown, the Mini All4 uses a BMW 3.0-litre diesel engine to provide power to all four wheels. The engine generates around 310 hp, which is controlled through a six-speed manual gearbox. Carrying up to 400 litres of fuel onboard, the All4 gave Dakar legend Stéphane Peterhansel his fourth and fifth car victories in 2012 and 2013.

A Touareg hurtles across desert trails. Twin shock absorbers on each wheel help keep the car gripping the ground as it climbs over the roughest terrain.

TOP FUEL DRAGSTERS
Ultimate speed demons

Drag racing pits two vehicles side-by-side on short, straight drag strips in National Hot Rod Association (NHRA) competitions in North America and in FIA-approved events elsewhere. Different classes of vehicle are involved, from drag bikes to funny cars with jacked-up, customized bodies. The fastest of all are Top Fuel dragsters. Their incredible acceleration (zero to 160 km/h in just 0.8 seconds) easily surpasses the fastest supercars.

The driver wears a fire-resistant racing suit, a neck collar to protect against G-forces and is strapped into the narrow cockpit in a five-point harness protected by a tubular roll cage.

Front canard wing deflects air, helping to force the small front wheels down onto the track.

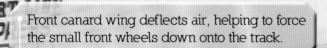

EXPLOSIVELY ENGINED

A Top Fuel dragster's large aluminium block engine runs on explosive fuel that consists of up to 90 per cent nitromethane. Superchargers ram air into the cylinders to help boost power. Each of the engine's eight cylinders generates more power than an entire NASCAR, and a Top Fuel's total engine can generate up to 8,000 hp – more than the first four rows of a Formula 1 starting grid or 50 family saloon cars.

TRANSMITTING POWER

All that explosive power has to be transmitted to the dragster's rear wheels, a process that takes just 15/100ths of a second. The vehicle is fitted with 91-cm-diameter tyres that are more than 40 cm wide. Before racing, a burnout is performed – the rear wheels are spun hard to warm the tyres and lay down a fresh patch of tyre rubber on the drag strip for extra grip.

A Top Fuel dragster can reach 450 km/h before you've finished reading this sentence! In 2005, a dragster driven by Tony Schumacher hit a record speed of 540.97 km/h.

SUDDEN SLOWDOWN

Racing over drag strips of 402 m (quarter mile) or 305 m (1,000 ft), Top Fuel dragsters can cross the finish line at 500 km/h or faster, and so require braking assistance. In addition to rear-wheel carbon disc brakes, drag chutes are released, creating large amounts of drag (air resistance) to slow the vehicle down.

The long, slim body has a maximum wheelbase of 7.62 m and is formed of magnesium alloy and carbon fibre. It is shaped to slice through the air.

FUTURE CARS

The car industry is 150 years old but is still developing and changing. Innovations continue as the industry never stands still. So what does the future hold? No one is certain, but there are some likely trends and advances. Concerns over pollution, climate change and the use of fossil fuels mean that future cars will be more energy efficient or use alternative fuels, while 3D printing and smart materials may enable radically new car shapes and designs. Finally, further advances in computing and sensors may lead to vehicle-to-vehicle (V2V) communications, enabling cars to cruise automatically without a human driver.

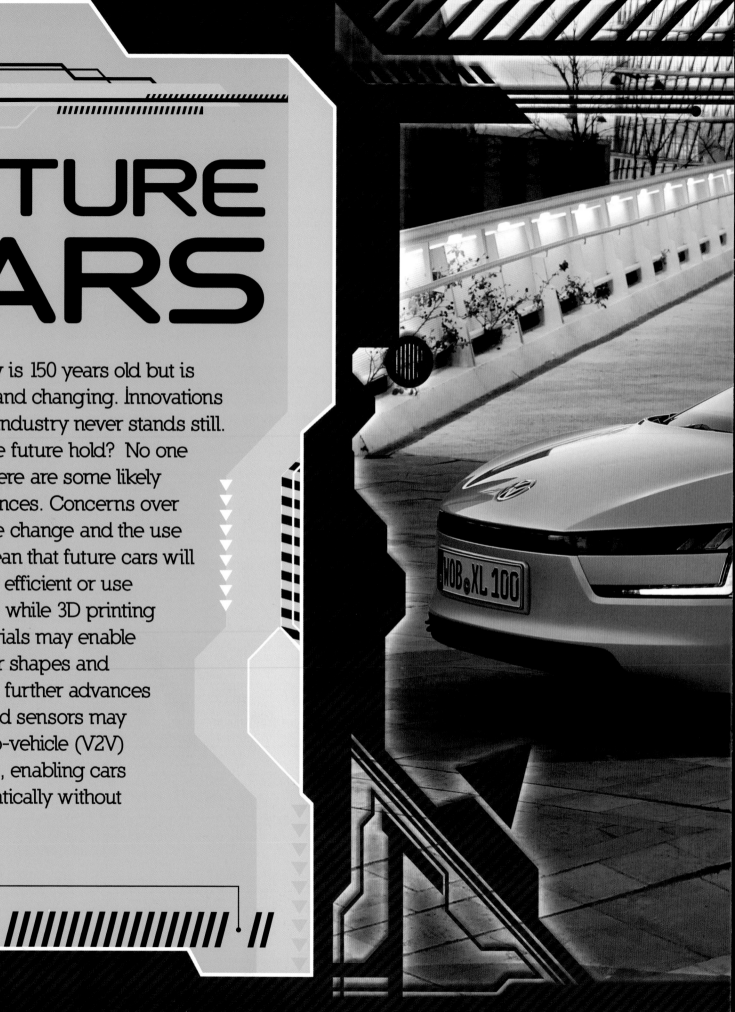

Volkswagen's XL1 is a narrow, teardrop-shaped hybrid car which is just 1.7 m at its widest and carries one passenger sitting behind the driver. Designed to be incredibly fuel efficient, the XL1 needs just 0.9 litres of diesel fuel to travel 100 km, equal to 310 miles to the UK gallon.

CONCEPT CARS
Off the drawing board

Concept cars are prototype machines, either models or working vehicles, built by car manufacturers to publicize their skills and engineering, to promote new technologies and ideas and to gauge opinion on new design directions. Some showcase technologies that car-makers feel may reach their production vehicles in the near future.

The Ford Nucleon concept proposed in 1958 did away with a petrol-driven engine in favour of a nuclear reactor driving a steam engine.

EARLY IDEAS

Harley Earl was one of the first concept car designers. His 1951 GM Le Sabre, with its tail fins and wrap-around windshield, influenced other car-makers' production models. GM's rival, Ford, constructed their own space-age-looking concept car, the Lincoln Futura, in 1955, complete with large body fins and clear bubble canopy. It didn't make it to production but the concept car was later turned into the Batmobile that starred in the 1966 *Batman* TV series.

The strikingly low and angular Stratos Zero was built by Italian designer Nuccio Bertone in 1970. It featured a hinged windscreen acting as the car door.

POSSIBLE OR IMPOSSIBLE?

Nissan's 2007 Pico 2 featured wheels that could turn in any direction, so the car could drive sideways. BMW's GINA (below) has no solid body panels. Instead, the car is covered in a stretchy spandex-like fabric. Underneath, a skeleton of wires moved by electric and hydraulic actuators can move the skin to change the vehicle's shape or unzip to reveal headlights.

FAR INTO THE FUTURE

Some vehicles provide glimpses of the distant future. Toyota's FV2 concept car, unveiled at the Tokyo Motor Show in 2013, asks whether wheels have to be at each corner. It places them in a cross formation around a plastic body pod that holds one person. The FV2 even dispenses with a steering wheel; the car would be driven instead by a person's body movements.

GINA's body can shift shape to 'grow' a rear spoiler when driving at high speeds.

The body skin moves to open the doors upwards. When the doors are shut, the skin is smooth and streamlined.

DIGITAL DRIVING
Truly smart cars

The latest cars are already packed with digital technology that makes driving easier, gives more control over the car or enables vehicles to monitor their performance. The vehicles can then alert the driver and garage should problems develop. Most experts predict that this is only the beginning, and that an era of truly smart, connected cars lies ahead.

In 2013, a Mercedes S500 Intelligent Drive car retraced the 100-km route taken by Bertha Benz from Mannheim to Pforzheim back in 1888. It made the entire journey without a human driver!

AT YOUR ASSISTANCE

New automatic driver aids include LED headlights, which detect oncoming traffic and adjust their beams so as not to dazzle other drivers. Some cars adjust the windscreen wipers or the volume levels of sound systems according to how fast the car is going. Future cars may not only monitor all of a car's key parts but also the driver, using cameras and other sensors to check that they are alert, that their eyes are open and focused on the road ahead, and that the car is not veering out of its lane.

BMW's ConnectedDrive features radars that sense the distance of vehicles ahead. It can override the driver's control of the brakes to keep speed down, as well as warning the driver about lane changing and sensing vehicles overtaking the car from behind.

CONNECTED CARS

Vehicle-to-Vehicle (V2V) systems may allow future cars to be in constant communication with one another via their in-car computers. Together, they could detect speed changes, traffic blackspots and road risks, and even allow driverless cruising on reserved lanes on motorways, keeping the cars a safe distance apart automatically.

SMART GLASS

Driver displays are getting more and more clever and future vehicles may feature windows and windscreens made of smart glass. All sorts of data can be projected onto the glass, from guide lines for parking in tight spaces to safe driving directions or a terrain map of the route ahead made by the car's laser rangefinders and night vision sensing systems.

GREEN MACHINES
Sustainable driving

With concerns about pollution and the future availability of fossil fuels such as oil, car manufacturers are developing technologies that use less fuel or obtain their energy from sustainable sources, such as solar power. Solar panels full of photovoltaic cells can convert sunlight into electricity to power electric motors in cars. Today, most solar-powered cars are experimental and feature in technology-proving races, but some production hybrid cars, such as the Ford C-Max Solar Energi, are being fitted with solar roof panels to top up their batteries and increase the cars' range.

The single-seat Tokai Challenger won the 2011 World Solar Challenge event over 2,998 km of Australian roads, covering the course at an average speed of 91.54 km/h.

Lightweight single-seat vehicles, such as this 300-kg Toyota i-Road, use less energy to get from A to B. Such vehicles could save millions of litres of fuel lost by people driving alone in much larger cars.

An array of 2,100 photovoltaic cells cover the Challenger's upper surface, converting sunlight into electricity to power the vehicle.

EVERY LITTLE HELPS

Car makers look at many ways to make cars more efficient, from improving aerodynamics to reducing weight. Stop-start engines, which cut out when a car is idling or stopped at traffic lights, can add 5 per cent fuel efficiency in urban driving. In 1991, the VW 'Umwelt' Golf was one of the first cars to have this feature. BMW have sold more than 500,000 cars with stop-start technology since 2006.

ALL-ELECTRIC DREAMS

More than three million hybrid cars have been sold in the United States alone, but all-electric vehicles are rarer. The best-selling all-electric car is the Nissan Leaf, more than 150,000 of which have been sold. Improvements in batteries may see lighter all-electric cars able to travel longer distances before needing to recharge. The Tesla all-electric Model S P85D boasts supercar performance. It accelerates from 0–96 km/h in just 3.2 seconds.

Detroit Electric's SP:01 has a top speed of 249 km/h – sensational for an all-electric car.

The 2015 Toyota FCV's hydrogen fuel cell enables the car to travel up to 700 km before needing to refuel.

FUTURE FUELS

Hydrogen fuel cells are devices that use a chemical reaction between hydrogen and oxygen to produce electricity, water and some heat, but no harmful emissions. Electric cars fitted with hydrogen fuel cells may become popular future cars, able to be refuelled in minutes rather than the hours needed to recharge conventional electric cars. However, expensive networks of hydrogen refuelling stations would need to be constructed.

Car manufacturers will continue to embrace what made them successful in the past but merge it with cutting-edge technology and new thinking in the future. The Mercedes Silver Lightning concept is a striking example. It features advanced innovations packed into a design that was inspired by the legendary W125 Silver Arrow racing cars of the 1930s.

Cockpit might be packed with futuristic driving aids, including driverless control and an option for the car to park itself.

MAGNETIC ROOF

Futuristic twists include a retractable roof system made of magnetic tiles that can be added or removed in seconds. The vehicle might be powered by a non-polluting, lightweight fuel cell driving high-efficiency electric motors, which move the car's omni-directional wheels. These feature rollers inside the rim, which can tilt in a range of directions to move the car sideways as well as forwards and back.

Sleek, low design would cut through the air well, reducing air resistance and fuel usage.

MERCEDES BENZ W125 SILVER ARROW

The most powerful racing car when it was built in 1937, the W125 held the title for over 30 years. Its giant engine weighed 222 kg, generated 596 hp and was supplied with fuel by an equally large 240-litre tank. The W125 propelled the car to speeds of over 300 km/h on the track, while a highly modified W125, the Rekordwagen (right), clocked a speed of 432.7 km/h along the A5 autobahn in 1938 – still the fastest speed ever recorded on a German autobahn.

The body of the car may be covered in tiny nano-cells that repel dirt. The cells may also work like solar cells, converting sunlight into electricity to power the car's electrics.

Bright, coloured lights run round the edge of the omni-directional wheels.

Future fuel-cell powered engine may be capable of travelling more than 1200 km before needing to stop and refuel.

GLOSSARY

ABS Antilock braking system. A computer-controlled system that prevents brakes from locking up and tyres from skidding.

Airbag A cushion that fills with gas when a major impact occurs to reduce a car occupant's chances of serious head or chest injury.

CAD/CAM Short for computer-aided design/computer-aided manufacturing, these are powerful computer systems that enable engineers to design cars and their parts.

Chassis The basic frame or structure of a car, to which other components are attached.

Concept car A vehicle built to demonstrate new vehicle designs or technologies.

Coupé A two-door, enclosed-body, hard-roofed car designed to seat two people in the front with up to two people in the back.

Downforce A force caused by the way air flows around a car, which helps push the car down onto the road.

FIA Short for the Fédération Internationale de l'Automobile, the organization that runs many of motorsport's biggest competitions.

Four-wheel drive A transmission system that provides power to drive all four wheels of a car.

Grip The ability of a vehicle's design, suspension, aerodynamics and tyres to hold the car on the road.

Handling How a car responds when driving, particularly to changes in speed and direction.

Hybrid cars Cars which have both an internal combustion engine and another drive system such as an electric motor.

Monocoque An all-in-one body design where the outer skin supports much of a vehicle's load instead of an internal frame.

NASCAR Short for National Association for Stock Car Auto Racing, a body that organizes the Sprint Cup series of track races for powerful saloon cars in the USA.

Piston A rod-shaped part that moves up and down inside an engine cylinder.

Power steering A system using hydraulics or electric motors to increase the force on the steering system, meaning the driver uses less effort to turn the steering wheel.

Roll cage A strong frame inside a car's cabin that protects the driver and passengers, especially if the car rolls over.

Sedan A four-door car with an enclosed boot area and with the full roof height running back to the rear seats.

Streamlined Shaped so that air flows easily over and around it.

Supercharger A device powered by a belt, gear, shaft or chain connected to the engine's crankshaft. It forces air into a car's engine in order to increase power.

Suspension The system of springs, shock absorbers and other components, directly connected to the wheels or the axles, that affect a car's handling and grip.

Telemetry A radio device that relays information from electronic sensors about a car's engine, tyres and other key components to a race team's base during testing or a race.

Transmission A system of gears and shafts which transmit power from the engine to the axles of the wheels.

Turbocharger A device that uses a turbine driven by exhaust gases from the engine to force air into an internal-combustion engine in order to increase engine power.

Valve (engine) An opening in an engine cylinder which opens and closes to let fuel and air in or gases out.

Wheelbase The distance between a car's front and rear axles.

Wings Aerodynamic devices, usually shaped like upside-down aircraft wings, which help generate downforce or improve handling.

Acknowledgements

The publishers would like to thank the following sources for their kind permission to reproduce the pictures in this book.

Key: t = Top, b = Bottom, c = Centre, l = Left & r = Right

1: Getty Images/Matt Sullivan; 2-3: LAT Photographic; 4-5: Porsche AG/© 2014 Porsche Cars North America, Inc.; 6: Getty Images/Rusty Jarrett; 6-7: Lamborghini/Automobili Lamborghini S.p.A.; 7: Rex Features/Andy Willsheer; 9t: Mercedes-Benz/Copyright Daimler © All Rights Reserved; 9c & 9b: Private Colleciton; 10: Shutterstock.com/Natursports; 11t: Rex Features; 11b: © 1994-2014 Koenigsegg. All rights reserved; 12: Getty Images/Tim Graham; 12-13 & 13r: Getty Images/Marco Prosch; 14-15 Getty Images/Sean Gallup; 15: Topfoto.co.uk/Ullstein Bild; 16-17: Corbis/Martyn Goddard; 18: Rex Features/AGF s.r.l.; 18-19: Porsche AG/© 2014 Porsche Cars North America, Inc; 19: Alamy/Oleksiy Maksymenko; 20: Alamy/epa european pressphoto agency b.v.; 20-21: Alamy Images/Motoring Picture Library; 21c: Alamy/Vario images; 21t: © BMW Group; 22: Rex Features/Magic Car Pics; 22-23: © Lamborghini/Automobili Lamborghini S.p.A.; 23: Alamy Images/Mark Bourdillon; 24: © Bugatti Automobiles S.A.S.; 24-25: Shutterstock/Max Earey; 25t, 25bc, 25br: © Bugatti Automobiles S.A.S. 26: Corbis/Transtock; 26-27: Alamy/WENN Ltd.; 27t: © Koenigsegg; 27c: Alamy/WENN Ltd; 28-29: Getty Images/Haruyoshi Yamaguchi/Bloomberg; 29t: Shutterstock/Vereshchagin Dmitry; 29r: Thinkstock/iStock; 30-31: Corbis/Car Culture; 32: Corbis/Hoch Zwei; 32-33: Porsche AG/© 2014 Porsche Cars North America, Inc.; 33t: Porsche AG /© 2014 Porsche Cars North America, Inc.; 33b: Shutterstock/TonyV3112; 34-35: Corbis/Don Heiny; 34: Shutterstock/Radoslaw Lecyk; 35t & 35c: Getty Images/Klemantaski Collection; 36-37: Volkswagen/© Copyright Volkswagen of America, Inc.; 36, 36-37, 37t: Volkswagen/© Copyright Volkswagen of America, Inc.; 37: Rex Features/c.W. Disney/Everett; 38-39: Corbis/Car Culture; 39t: Corbis/Bryan Smith/ZUMA Press; 39b: David J. Griffin/Icon SMI; 40, 40-41, 41: Mercedes-Benz/Copyright Daimler © All Rights Reserved.; 42-43, 42c, 42t: © Lamborghini/Automobili Lamborghini S.p.A.; 43b: Getty Images/Klemantaski Collection; 44: Getty Images/Chris Ware/Keystone Features/Hulton Archive; 44-45: Getty Images/Hubert Fanthomme/Paris Match; 45b: Getty Images/Darrell Ingham; 45t: Getty Images/Keystone-France/Gamma-Keystone; 46-47: Rex Features/Andy Willsheer; 48-49: Shutterstock/Art Konovalov; 49t: Rex Features/Andy Wilman; 49b: Private Collection; 49c: Peel Engineering; 50: Alamy/Oleksiy Maksymenko; 51: Alamy/pbpgalleries; 52: Gibbsamphitrucks.com; 52-53: © Watercar Inc.; 53t: Terrafugia Inc.; 53c: Getty Images/Simon Dawson/Bloomberg; 54: Getty Images/ISC Images & Archives; 54-55: Getty Images/Dan Dennison; 55: Rex Features/Sipa Press; 56: Getty Images/Jonathan Moore; 58-59: Getty Images/Patrick Smith; 60: Getty Images/Micke Fransson/AFP; 60-61: Getty Images/William West/AFP; 61: Alamy/Russell Hunter; 62: Getty Images/Peter Fox; 62-63: LAT Photographic/Andy Hone; 63t: LAT Photographic/Charles Coates; 64: © 2014. AUDI AG. All rights reserved; 64-65: LAT Photographic/Jeff Bloxham; 65: LAT Photographic/Alastair Staley; 66-67: Corbis/Martin Zabala/Xinhua Press; 67: Shutterstock.com/Rodrigo Garrido; 68-69: Corbis/Marc Sanchez/Icon SMI; 69t: Corbis/Chris Williams/Icon SMI; 69c: Getty Images/Rusty Jarrett; 70-71: Mercedes-Benz/Copyright Daimler © All Rights Reserved.; 72: Corbis/Car Culture; 72-73, 73c: © BMW Group; 73t: Shutterstock.com/Thampapon; 74-75: Mercedes-Benz /Copyright Daimler © All Rights Reserved.; 75t: Alamy Images/Jim West, 75r; Getty Images/Coneyl Jay; 76: Getty Images/Jean-Pierre Clatot/AFP; 76-77: Getty Images/Mark Kolbe; 77t: Detroit Electric; 77b Getty Images/Kazuhiro Nogi/AFP; 78-79, 79: Mercedes-Benz /Copyright Daimler © All Rights Reserved.